ruined stars

Wonderful Lynn
with ♡ + more ♡
xo RW xo

ruined stars
poems by RM Vaughan

MISFIT

ECW PRESS

Published by ECW PRESS
2120 Queen Street East, Suite 200, Toronto, Ontario, Canada M4E 1E2

NATIONAL LIBRARY OF CANADA CATALOGUING IN PUBLICATION

Vaughan, R. M. (Richard Murray), 1965–
Ruined stars / R.M. Vaughan.

Poems.
ISBN 1-55022-675-4

I. Title.

PS8593.A94R84 2004   C811'.54   C2004-902602-X

Editor: Michael Holmes/a misFit book
Cover and Text Design: Darren Holmes
Cover photo: Scott McEwan
Production and Typesetting: Mary Bowness
Printing: Gauvin Press

This book is set in Goudy.

The publication of *Ruined Stars* has been generously supported by the Canada Council, the Ontario Arts Council, the Ontario Media Development Corporation, and the Government of Canada through the Book Publishing Industry Development Program. **Canadä**

DISTRIBUTION
CANADA: Jaguar Book Group, 100 Armstrong Avenue, Georgetown, ON, L7G 5S4

PRINTED AND BOUND IN CANADA

ECW PRESS
ecwpress.com

Contents

UNIVERSAL PICTURES

6 POEMS FOR ALEISTER CROWLEY

LONDON AFTER MIDNIGHT

ACKNOWLEDGEMENTS

To the handsome and talented Michael Holmes, who makes everything possible, many thanks and much love. To "Uncle Jack" David, queen maker, many thanks. To Andrew Harwood and Scott McEwan, cover model and cover photographer, many thanks. To William and Anne Forrestall, cherished friends, many thanks. To the Toronto, Ontario and Canada Councils, many thanks.

The poem sequence "6 Poems for Aleister Crowley" is greatly indebted to Lawrence Sutin's excellent *Do What Thou Wilt: A Life of Aleister Crowley*.

Similarly, Jared Mitchell provided a fountain of knowledge (and occasional scolding) during a trip to Palm Springs, from which the poems "Palm Springs Stories" were hatched, and James BL Hollands squired me around the labyrinth that is London — a great help when I wrote the poems in "London After Midnight."

Everything else I made up.

Cover photograph of Andrew Harwood's "Miss Teen Georgian Bay 1987" performance by Scott McEwan, from McEwan's 2003–04 photo-series *Social Devastasia*. Reproduced courtesy of the artist.

Interior illustrations by William Forrestall, from the 2000 series "British Museum."
Reproduced courtesy of the artist.

Author photo by Paul Forsyth.

Early versions of a handful of the poems in this collection have appeared in *The Fiddlehead, Taddle Creek, Xtra!, Mix Magazine, rabble.ca, Descant, Double-Double*, the anthologies *Coastlines: The Poetry of Atlantic Canada* and *The Common Sky: Canadian Writers Against the War*, as well as the chapbook *An Herbal for Men*, co-produced with Allyson Mitchell.

Author's Note

"Conversations with Will" was originally written for *The Fiddlehead*, as part of a project that paired poets with visual artists. I was lucky to be paired with William Forrestall, a good friend and a great painter. Anyone who knows Will also knows that he is an avid conversationalist, to say the least. The poems are an indirect record of our conversations, of me watching him work in his studio, and of his genius.

For Dorothy Vaughan

Palm Springs Stories
For Jared Mitchell

PALM SPRINGS INTERNATIONAL AIRPORT

Is surrounded by coyotes, brown skunk-dogs   living on pizza crusts, dropped hot dogs
martini olives, waste water from airplanes   whatever's left
I want to pet one, but remember I came here to get away from scroungers, from bad men

So, this is probably another love poem   Few are not   I, or he himself   *(the object)*
will ply open this not especial meeting of thread and glue and, say, Irish rag (2 pd weight)
   I do not decide my stock, *yet*   this right angle where information and chewed tree
and silk agree   *the signature*   and nod, smirk, cough, think he knows everything

go to Hell
                        I am not done lying   and he never stopped

All autobiography is travelogue, map play   some of us just get around more

   our beds are plains, prickly transvaals dotted with hoofed traffic   beasts
with nautilus horns, seven legs, recessed fangs (or wings)   plus voles, racing
                                             headfirst in the underbrush   humble as lint
   our beach towels are as telling as dirty cafeteria trays, where monsters pool & flick
in the wet corners   crusty and smelling of sour wheat
   our clothes, stained & obvious as newspapers, commingle & knot   make waffled
pyramids, cotton pagodas, damp lighthouses manned by dust mites

Whatever we own or caress or breathe on or slurp or pick at or bump against or visit or
waste   tells on us, spills the beans, makes with the goods, testifies   so
      I thrush to print, I publish and perish

In Dynastic Egypt, words were procreative   carve "snake" into a basalt block, a wall
of crisped mud or a palm trunk & expect hisses, blinding spit   expect diamond heads
and pulsing chevrons   the Carpet Viper the Spotted Night Adder the Bandy-Bandy
the Mulga the Lisping Krait the Rinkhal   any black and twitching scourge

we know so little magic now

CALIENTE TROPICS HOTEL

A timeline:

"caliente"   Spanish for hot, for scalding and, later, for Indian   thousands of Indians
met on orange desert paths, found sleeping under spiny, fat barrel cactus   by generals
and Madrid foot soldiers looking for giants or headless man tigers   generals who dipped
their olive faces and twisted, boot sore ankles in the salty, bubbling streams   and ran
screaming   chased by Indian laughter, low and curling

later, a priest named Almedo or Almondo or Alberto   watched the Indian women dunk
their babies in the whistling hot springs & ran away & wrote: the females boil
   their children alive
            and wrap their cooked hides in thorns   meaning: I cannot tell one Indian baby
from another, and the women wear no covering

but the Caliente are gone   what can one expect?   the babies of the babies
of the babies of many generations more of the famous boiled babies   own casinos
and cab companies   and hide from their neighbours   (behind parked cars and bushy
tulip trees they dart & duck   flashes of graying pigtails or beaded suede   faces brown
as geckos)   But everything is named after the losers: the Caliente Fairway
(golf) the Caliente Coooler (peppered vodka) a Caliente steak (thin as a splinter, salted
with lime) nine Caliente Super Savers (drug stores) one Caliente Critters (tropical fish &
kittens)   the Hot Rocks Indian Massage
and my motel, The Caliente Tropics   (2 stories, one pool, pink and lemon stucco trim,
cleaned by Mexicans)

Mexicans too young (or too smart) to remember the bad years, the decade of Mr. Kenneth
and Miss Sante   Mr. and Mrs. Kimes   famous hoteliers, drinkers & Democrats
who greeted their guests in pale summer wools & Hermes espadrilles

(he always wore blue, one housemaid told the jury, baby blue   Mr. Kenneth, he
walked around the pool every morning, early, in that blue shirt   the water had to match
or else, because Mr. Kenneth he always says)

    The Kimes Hotel Promise: Cleanliness   fair prices   quiet staff and a nice view
    meaning: invisible women carrying soap, ice, newspapers, soft drinks   French rubbers
in bruised hands   women who slept in locked basements, on damp mattresses packed
with silverfish   who paid for once a week showers, ate dry corn sandwiches and warm
Coke for supper   endured Sante's telephone cord whip & Mr. Kenneth's special lady tax

          at her trial, Sante told the judge "different people learn differently"
meaning: I cannot tell one Mexican from another

ten years later, free on bail   Sante Kimes smothered an Arab banker in the Bahamas
shot a car dealer in LA   buried alive a drifter in Nevada   strangled a millionaire
widow   got 100 years to life   & was played by Mary Tyler Moore on television

Thousand Palms Canyon

An inelegant clutter of sooty husks, of palm trees as fat and untended as widows   upside
down chandeliers, newspaper mobiles   the canyon
droops and slinks   down into the bent, gravelly hills   a moist fold   a blot
   remarkable only because it's wet, and low   and minutes from town   (where
palms are skinned of old leaves & wired into West Point postures, their bark sun-cured
      to black & cross-hatched like whip braids   Flintstone palms, tufted swizzle sticks lit
with fairy lights)

         My buddy plays Kim Novak in *Vertigo*, caresses a crusty palm with both hands
fakes a trance, repeats Madeline's haunted redwood reverie   *I was born here . . .*
somewhere here I died
   but it doesn't work   a palm tree is not a redwood, a boulder is not a
church spire, or the Golden Gate   the stakes are lower here   & I am too fat
to be Jimmy Stewart   I did not pack a blue dress, a Spanish emerald necklace
      and there are lizards, scaly harlequinos   a thousand green and black lizards
the size of dollar bills jumping from tree to tree   giggling

40 feet down, in the deepest cut in the earth, the quiet spooks us   even the lizards stop
sucking gnats from ponds, stop investigating the dust
      nothing hunts, nothing is alert

we brush between filthy fronds, sneezing, malarial   two Schliemanns, in Rayon
determined to see the lowest point, the first growth   a burred congestion of damp
and sand, grit and vegetable   to see where trunk curls with trunk and roots cord the path
hard as railway ties   the slow violence of rot

THE TOOL SHED BAR, EAST SUNNY DUNES

A legend, from 1977

Dinah Shore is in a hurry   Her diary reads
        Golf at San Lorenzo, salmon soup, massage and Sidecars at 4, Dolores Hope
showing off a Chinese actress, unpronounceable   up for a Globe or a Ceasare or won
something already at Cannes   waved in by the board, of course, just this once
       Imelda, of course, always Imelda, and Mrs. Wasserman (bad back again) with Mrs.
Lemmon   and Mrs. Ford, Mrs. Malden (cancer?) Stephen Boyd — not working, Irene
Dunne (after Mass), Mrs. Lynde (Paul — haha!) and so-and-so from Salt Lake, fortune in

        her car stalls, 11 miles from anywhere   6 yards from The Toolshed
she spots a coyote behind a cantina and bolts   Inside,
the bar is cool and dim   men lean, legs out, shoulders flat on black tar walls   cowboys
marines, motorcycle enthusiasts, police officers (thank God!)   sun lovers and retirees

Hello boys!
A phone is found   A complementary Manhattan mixed   Miss Shore, a chair?

    Now, boys, here's the situation — I'm already 20 minutes late and the car's   well,
who knows about cars these days, all Japanese   (everyone nods)   and Triple A needs 40
minutes to get here   and then there's my hair

Ken, 20 years in hair   6 feet and 5, leather master   removes his Muir cap
Miss Shore, a stool? A Marine pulls up his tank top, sniffs the pits and smiles

    Miss Shore removes her jacket, drapes her front in white cotton   the Marine winks
scissors, an olive skewer, ice cube tongs and KY are found   Ken takes only a moment,

it seems   faster than five swigs, a pop song, lunch at Roddy's (haha!)
Master Ken refuses the folded 20, takes a kiss instead   walks Miss Shore to her taxi

3 years later, Dinah Shore will campaign for Ronald Reagan   President Reagan
will not say the word AIDS in public   until 1988, until Rock, until Andy &
after Ken, dead by '84

Joshua Tree National Park

If I say, again   It's just like the Roadrunner cartoon!
            (granite cuddling sandstone   rocks — no, monoliths — as big as malls
pirouetting on slim stems of compressed dust   the impossibly relaxed gravity)
  it's because I'm from an ocean town, a coast   a washed away place
        because I have never seen anything so permanent, dusty   so silly
    because my reference points for Beauty are all tidal   expansive, sweeping, turbulent
not playful   and it's a shock to be charmed by upside down rocks

The real roadrunners are a let down — even I could catch one
      Their legs are stubbed, thorn-knuckled   two dirty pipe cleaners holding up
a bread basket of feathers, baseball glove brown
    & cardboard matte   (about as exotic, as tropical, as starlings, robins or chickadees)
    and, they won't run away
    won't make helicopter blade spirals, gyro whirs
dust plumes or saucy faces   *won't move*

I've met smarter animals   been foxed by pollywogs, jellyfish, ladybugs
  creatures without spines, synapses, skeletons or ears   shown the door
  by sleep-starved lovers, clerks unencumbered by conscience or reading   old women &
fog-wanderers, simple folk and ghosts

But here, where dagger flowers cut my ankles, where briar trees lunge
at my elbows and ribs   under a startling sun, the always needling threat of stroke
  this bird, too stupid to fly, only wonders why I'm not baring my teeth
  for the kill

VE1XE

I

My first alphabet, this code   melodic and martial, a signature for a sergeant
or pilot, wartime correspondent   man of adventure   not a nervous parent, home
short wave HAM radio enthusiast, child-man with boy hobbies
not a father

I learned this sequence, this double-E near-palindrome   before "hungry," before "cat"
because it was all I heard him say   after silent dinners, when I wanted sleep, my father
chanted numbers and letters into the same night sky that scared me
signed his encrypted name into the air, reduced himself to particles
& waves, sparked dust   and me to less

2

He had admirers, of course   VEIXE collected "handles" & "stations"
his legion of invisible pals, acronym-friends   global lonely hearts with absent wives,
subdued children   patient pets   a telegraphic syndicate of idle chatterers   all men

postcards, smudged by untidy sorters and foreign rains, insulated his office
Rhodesia, West Germany, Ukraine, Luxembourg, Ceylon, Gibraltar, Qatar   coveted
elsewheres   too far to visit, see in person   smell or touch or remember   commit to

my men, at least   get kisses, a pinch for luck, cold germs, skin flakes

& Dad and I are neck and neck
in numbers

3

3 years before he died (in his sleep, in his bed, full of Postum and Atavan   just the way
he wanted it   *he always got what he wanted)*   in a night terror
Murray pulled the station to a shell   sent cables and plugs, wires, tubes, microphones
amps, jacks & cords   away, sold for a tenth

but kept the casings, the black and chrome hulls, in neat array
made a mini charcoal Habitat   a doll house city for Mom to dust
and played "radio" every Wednesday
went from removed to imaginary, aloof to mad   from disembodied affection   to fakery

How familiar   I thought, the original test case
forgetting to offer thanks for distraction   the balm of the unloved

my last words to him   *are you dead yet?* (our old joke)   he answered No
        I'm not in bed

Conversations with Will

I

down here   (in Ali Baba's basement)

under
       a dozen plus topographies of autumn
       squash, teak chests, glazed toys, treasures
       of broken glass

     behind
  the casual rows of paint pots   of blues, yellows, greens, cleansing ivories

flush against the hairs
of a hundred unnamed animals
  oiled, bound, and impaled   neatly
on enameled sticks

my feet trace
a thin crevasse   in the cement
        (wall to wall)
dividing   resentment from
gratitude   "inspired" from
bored   paint from camera
the patience of the saints
from mania

I've watched you walk away from the TV
and return — play record after record to an empty
room   tune five radios to the same station and still hunt
for information in the shiny, curled weeklies piled high

in the sun porch

what are you hearing   besides the scratch
of bristle on board?

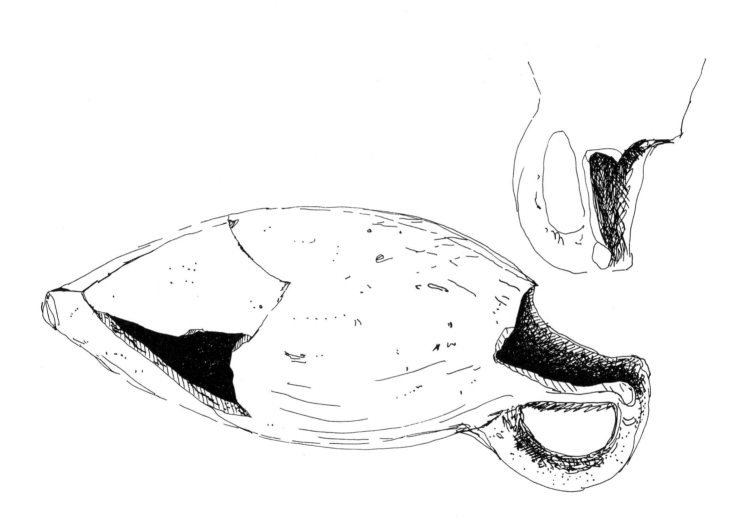

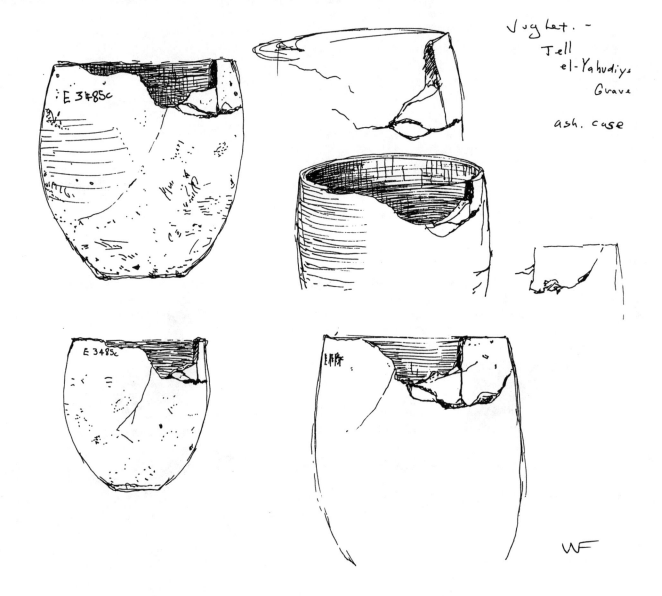

Juglet. –
Tell
el-Yahudiya
Grave

ash. case

E 3485c

E 3485c

WF

2

A temperament for looking
you call it

A decision to stare, blankly, for hours
at something you care nothing about
        you name it   (for hours?)

                until, your wrist itches and
        a quick prick of yellow paint (spit size) lands over a grid
behind a line   true to form
through the hollow of illustration

A gentle occupation, you smirk

    but lately, Willy, I can see colours charging
over your forehead

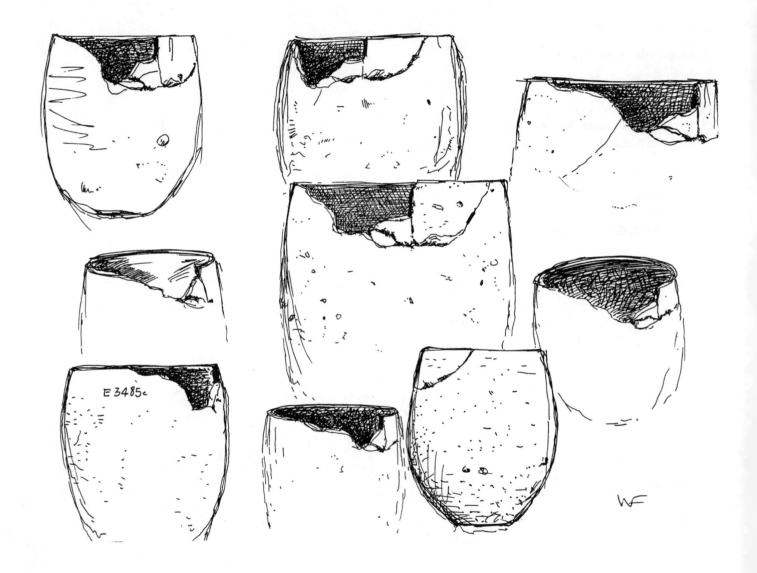

E 3485c

WF

3

Honestly now, don't you ever want to erase

muddy up the bond stock, burn the whole
lot   *run amok*
smear your white-white chest in cobalts and ochres
grow a ponytail and howl?

Really?
    well, everything's been done before, once
you look at it that way

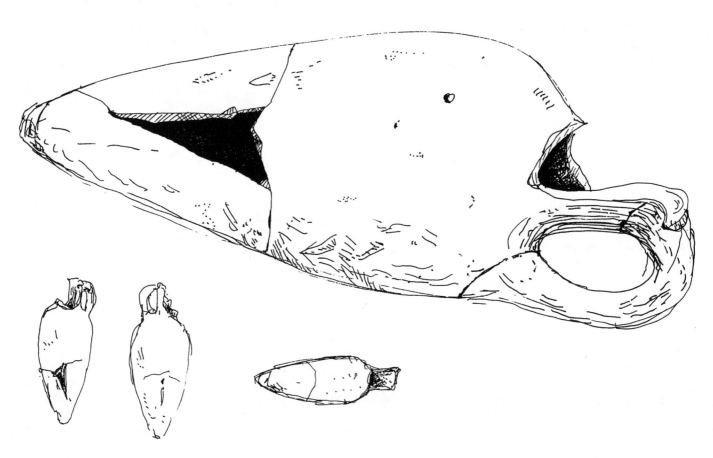

4

(I don't know about you) But
I'm tired of running around, spending my days
absorbing, absorbing, absorbing

being smart and unhappy at the same time

It's too much, it makes my hair gray it keeps me up at night it makes me eat
more than I want to
it drowns out the me in things

simple things, the stink of an apple   the weight of a full mug
the heartlessness of the cold air when I walk
home or —

Yes, that *Me*, that *conceit*   is just Desire
        sure, but   who doesn't want the world?

An Herbal for
Men Who Live Alone

Feverfew

A carbolic, the favourite of Saint Tomasa   who lined her potter's cauldron
     with crisped petals, her stomach with lye and scalded primrose   A tingling root
chewed for luck, longevity, against dry spleen or night terrors, in mah-jong heats
     This baby's clover, too bitter for nursing mothers   bruises with pinching
  (as do most bullies)   the damp switches of fan leaves   like green coins, hundreds per
stem   crease, remember touch (as do you)

take some in the morning, steeped in Korean corn husk tea   swallow absently
without sugar and quickly   to the flat back of the tongue — the dead, cold insensate patch
before the throat, a muscled plain meant to catch choking biscuits, balls of gristle, lies —
because anything so in discord with everything you love (sweetness, bulk, artificiality)
must be improving (like exercise or books about science)   will exact more than it adds
  eliminate, eliminate, eliminate   you repeat, for bravery   then swirl the mess, the
crushed forest, the pulpy runes   and squint, tilt, swallow, repeat   imagine
a bed shared 4 legs, 4 arms waking up uncovered weekend & garden plans his name

MINT

Eight spears   cut in threes, gloss side down   set in your shoes
between toes and sole, sock and leather   will hold the planter, bind him
     your woodsman, the rake   to you, his nose to your heel   for five days, four
nights & one long walk in any civic park   (the kind spattered with sore-red impatiens,
cleomes sticky as rope weed, fleecy, tired dog roses, dull and broken grass   lazy flowers
brought in trucks and planted with pole shovels, never touched by gardeners' hands)

washed in a bowl with lead shavings, frost-fattened currents & coils of hair (his hair)
1 year later   the leaves stain blue, false ink   azure as a gas flame, as wet platinum
eaten with orange peel and ginger, the leaves taste only of salt, of yellowed skin
& argument   and must be chewed & spat out twice, onto newspaper   else you're lost
wrapped in vine leaves, the mint will kill any houseplant or mouse, anything weak
but, tied with amber thread, steamed quills or half a shoelace (his lace) in two bunches
of twelve cuttings & hung from two trees — one bending north, one east — the cures attract
finches, hatchling gulls, maimed crows   & burn their pebbly gullets, in sympathy

Variegated Ivy

On St. Stanislaus Day (holy to *He Who Died Incorrupt*)   or in any drizzle   pinch
a trident leaf from its cord, brutally, to trap the juice   & hang it upside down
forks to the earth . . .   seven weekends after this severance   the white tips, the dried ivory
frills, have curled to a pale ochre   full of arrested chlorophyll   & revenge
      slice off the brown & crush the crackling specks in a bronze plate rubbed with sea salt
& cactus spines & throw the powder under the centre of your bed   *the hot spot*

he whispers as boys do — boys crowded limb on leg in tents lit by penlights   boys
in movie theatres bored by love scenes, exposition or landscape   boys in libraries,
boys on buses hobbled by fat ladies — whispers, between kisses, puckers, bites   *so*
warm you are so warm   down here   right here   Know then that you have won
Because, after, in the cooling   nothing he owns, remembers, plays with, covets or cleans
matches the red flush of your thighs, the sparks off your smallest hairs (snuffed wicks)
the first rubbery wet (like the cave of a cat's ear) before the clutch of your lowest, least
admirable organ (a hot blood sock), your patient radiance   *the bedevilment* & the comfort

Star Anis

A Russian cure for nightmares, bitter beer, lake distemper and dust cough   the 8 points
set in a cork bowl of blooded vinegar & aligned counter to the sun's crawl, to nature
will melt   turn to rusty mush, to spoiled bark soft as milk bread, as plums in October
     a collapsed star   tease out the hub, the wet pulp, with new silver needles   and daub
the left corners of his eyelids with brown rosettes   jealous bindis the colour of shit
of whining, shrill cicada wings, the bottoms of slippers   of domesticity & routine

the work-a-day colours you chose for sheets   are no longer calming & smell of old sugar
caked ink wells, warmed tin   of black toffee & other men's jizz (stranger funk)   key
rings he keeps secret, never jangles   *go through his pockets*   of medicines and breath
mints   Bury them   find a vacant lot & clear a triangle in the lowest corner   the hollow
     knead orange mountain ash berries, a newspaper from his birthday, 8 red candles &
your urine into a ball   make a knotted purse with his best pillowcase, in each twist place
one anis seed soaked in kerosene (embalmers' tea)   whisper your shared address & heave
the charm, this liar's sachet, backwards into the muddy keep   opposite you   him   & him

Maltese Cross

A misnomer, it is neither of Malta nor Christ   The roots are chewed by Mohammedan &
desert Jew   to prevent rape, house fire, loss of limbs & invasion   The die-off
the shriveled stalks   are mulched with pine nut hulls and cast over offal (human and
other) as fly chase   You need only a high summer's branch — 18 flowers, stamens &
petals red as rash, as chaffed thighs — blanched in boiled ink to milk purple, dusted
with ground Manitoba cactus paddles   to finish him, The Betrayer, The Quisling   lover

and now for the body, once shared   Dip two fingers in salted, warm wax   smooth
his elbows, knees, forehead, palms   plug his nostrils, ear canals, anus   untie him, lest
he convulse, attract lightning   and arrange him in disarray, *pieta mala fide*, under
a yellow lamp   Wait for gray moths, jumping moss spiders, curious winds, water
from his thumbs, death   In Deir el-Medineh, mothers of sons who will not be fathers ply
this charm on the fey, the flowery, on men who linger in arcades   to protect their sons
from joy   Let him feel nothing but stings, as you felt   Let him know nothing but shade,
madding clouds, obscure hues, distrust & cataracts   as you knew, in his corrupted arms

Sweet Woodruff

Only the first flowers will do, the mid-May pearl whites — later flourishes turn musty,
clot and blister like wet mothballs, like old rose oil   scald the skin   Only the first flowers
— those same pin daisies once beaten to cold balm by the lovers of Marsyas The Satyr
musician and bugger, flayed alive by the gods — will tame him, bring him to heel (or
hoof)   It takes only a tickle: three petal pricks under the balls and a lick of spit (for luck)
plus a swipe of ground red ant paste (for obedience)   to break him, reverse your role

Take him into the sunlight   He will complain of itches, bites, unexplained bubbles of hair
and pus, in-growth, hotfoot, white wens   then, grit in the bed, like diamonds   Offer to rub
him in coleus water, maltose and lamb's ear wool   the food of slugs, *Beggar's Salve*
bring him a wristlet of madder, five frozen brown eggs (armpit, armpit, sole, sole,
forehead) lengths of apple skin, anything cool and rotten   until he bucks at your touch
recognizes your particular pressure, even behind glass, galvanized rubber, dirty china
plate   until his hide is vaporous, until he can smell with his skin   Now pounce
trunk to trunk, belly to bowel, nipple to tooth   imprint, press, gravure burn, enshroud   own

Thai Basil

Clutters balconies in Bangkok   rows of Royal Yellow octagonal pots, agreed to garner money, attract augural beasts (lemurs, bats, speckled moths large as frying pans)   save babies from blindness . . . but, enough ethnography — pinch off the flower tops and burn the perfumed seed cones in a charcoal pit   Strip the stems, separate the olive & burgundy leaves   *earth and sky, dirt and cloud*   on a white sheet washed with lye, with his lucky socks & make two points — East green, to the old and forgotten   West purple, in hope

Wait for night air, an old moon and ice   Under a paramatta tent, a simple stick and cloak pyramid embroidered with numbers in white yarn — his birth date, address, blood sugar index — pound the dried leaves, rank with licorice-sweet oil, in a tub of tabby ordure   add white nicotina, for colour & *jumby*-scare   bundle handfuls of the mess into drawstring purses no bigger than his fist, or spleen (reverse sachets)   and hide the trickling loot bags beneath his front step, bedroom window & oldest tree   tie 5 to the front axle of his car mail one to his favourite restaurant   feed the rest to his dog   trespass, break and conjure until the world around him hums, is hazy with besetment & regret   the stink of you, gone

6 Performance Poems

Gay's Anatomy

Stomach

Let's start from the middle, from a soft place. The paunch, the tummy, the gut. I never want to hear the word abdominal again as long as I live. Taut stomachs are sexy on cats, not men. Let my men be dogs — sloppy, big pawed, pot bellied dogs. Faithful and dumb. When I tickle his warm centre, let the ends of my fingers sink, disappear. If I need to file my nails, I'll buy an emery board. If I need to bounce a dime, I'll find a hospital bed. Flat midriffs, like thin ice, cannot be trusted.

Thigh

Where, precisely, are the thighs? Oh, I know, I know — the top part of the leg. But where do thighs begin, end? Is everything above the knee a thigh, everything below the cock? And why do I need to know? Like most boys, every now and then I need to be dandled, tickled, play horsey. But after a certain age — say, 13 — and I am long, long after that uncertain age, a man has to be careful where he rests his hind quarters. I've broken my share of bamboo garden chairs, tested the tendons of more than one lap. A thigh might support me, a kneecap will not. Forget even trying a shin. But a thigh, a firm plank of muscle, will hold me. Long enough.

Neck

The back of the neck is a study in proportion, scale, and good taste. Too much neck, and you're kissing Plastic Man, making pillow talk with Don Knotts, on a date with Shelly Duvall. Too little neck, and you've got nothing to grab. Imagine your man is saving you from drowning (this happens more than metaphorically) and at that pivotal moment (the last gulp, your third time into the drink) you reach out for a neck to wrap your fingers around, a desperate life line, and all you get is skull. Slick, round skull. To the briny bottom you go. The problem with necks is, you can't tell a good one from the front. A strong chin makes up for a stumpy neck, and giraffes often shrug. The truth lies in the distance between the hairline and the spine — that bristly plain (so nice three days after a shave), that rectangle of flesh (pink in summer, wrapped and collared in winter), that stretch of skin half an inch makes, or marks.

Fingers

A lot of fags have a lot of ideas about fingers. I need not list the obvious. Admit it, you've been to those parties — the kind where some clown comes up behind you, swipes the crack of your ass and then makes everybody smell his foul, gnarled claws. Oh, the hilarity! Fingers are for bums like forks are for rum balls or steaming pie crusts. . . . Acknowledge the finger's role in your life, and then do like Smokey Robinson and Shop Around. Accept no nail biters. What's he so nervous about? And not too many rings, please, for safety reasons. Perfumed hand cream is a bad sign — not of femininity, but eczema. Fingers the size of snow shovels are good for rough stuff, but who's going to pull out your slivers, knit you a scarf? A piano player makes a good explorer, a guitar player a good tickler, and bongo drummers will give you a bit of colour where you need it least. Any man who works with his hands all day will do the same in bed, all night. Lady Chatterley was right.

Armpit

There are 33,876 items on the internet relating to male armpits. That's a lot of lifting and stretching and deodorizing (or not) and shaving (or not) and just plain thinking, thinking really hard, about a part of the body meant to be ignored. Like the appendix, the armpit has no evident use. Sure, pits connect the arm to the body, but wouldn't a belly button or a nipple be better than a gaping pocket, a mere cavity, the wound that will not hedge? My theory about armpits is that we developed the holes when we were monkeys, to hide our macadamia nuts and tasty lice, or maybe to ward off predators (perhaps the hair was fire alarm red, like a baboon's ass, or toxic orange, like a monarch butterfly's wings). But now we're the predators, our food is kept in cans and fridges, and the only thing we need to ward off is, well, 33,876 web sites about armpits. Evolution is so slow.

Forearm

A final word on forearms. The forearm is the only part of your body any skinny ass queen in a nightclub will ever admire for being wide. Cultivate your forearms as you might tobacco bushes or summer basil — plants admired for their broad, generous leaves. Set your great and manly shields atop any bar, handy fence post or brass rail and watch the dithering dollies rush toward you like figure skaters to a frozen pond. Let them slick your muscled flanks with their pouting little lips, break their sand blasted teeth on your ulna. Then step back, flex, scratch your elbows, yawn and walk away.

7 Steps To a Better Artist Statement

1. Know your audience. Who actually reads artist statements? Art students (first year), middle aged housewives taking Art Appreciation classes, and your parents. In other words, no-one who counts. So, relax. The Canada Council will not send a *gendarme d'exhibition* to the gallery to see your show, let alone to read the handful of paragraphs tacked to the wall by the door. And curators only read British and American art magazines, to steal ideas. You might as well have fun with your statement. Nobody else will.

2. Sincerity is the new irony. Mock manifestos, surrealist rants, comic strips, and concrete poems are outdated, and tell the reader that you don't take your work seriously, which is fine when you're 22 and still live at home. Think of your artist statement as a diary, as an Oprah book, as the sacred confessional. Dapple the lurid sentences with your hot tears. Tell us about your sex life, your eating disorders, your nascent homosexuality, why you grind your teeth. At the very least, it will be much funnier.

3. If your artist statement includes phrases like "occluding the performative absence," or, worse yet, "subjectivising the topology of place-ness," or, my all time personal favourite, "unstable narrative sites," you are eligible for the death penalty in 22 US states and a small tin medal in France. What the hell are you talking about? You don't really know, do you? Well, guess what: neither does anybody else. Confusing people is one thing — even, at times, an admirable choice — but admitting to your audience that you actually have no idea why you made the art in the first place is just stupid and self destructive. If you want to write bad prose, go teach at York University. Or take up novel writing (it worked for me).

4. Recycle, recycle, recycle. If you liked your last artist statement, there's no reason not to use it again. Nobody read the damned thing the first time around (see Step 1), so you won't get caught. And God knows your art hasn't changed. Lenin said it best: Originality is a bourgeois obsession.

5. Quote a passage from an important work of fiction. I've done this, and it works like a charm. Nothing adds weight and meaning to a wall full of pointless scribbles or dull paintings of parking lots than, say, Proust's gooey memories of his aunt's foot odor (for homosexual artists), a couple of love-starved paragraphs from Alice Munro

(feminist artists), or the latest bit of race-baiting from Louis Farrakhan (artists of colour). Why lose sleep worrying if your art has depth when you can simply borrow all the resonance you need from the bottomless, echoing well of classic literature? If you're determined to paint your childhood pain away, a little V.C. Andrews reads better than a whole lot of you.

6. It must not take longer to read your artist statement than it takes to look at your art. Proportion is everything. Here's a simple art-to-text ratio you can follow. One work in a big group show = no statement. A handful of works in a small group show = 3 paragraphs. Half of a two-person show = one page, but use a large font. Solo show = one page and a half or one small brochure with pictures. Retrospective in a museum . . . you'll be dead by then.

7. Silence is golden. Silence in the art world is good publicity. If all else fails, remain a mystery. You've already given the public your art — now they want your thoughts too? Greedy little shits. All you do is give, give, give. Refusing to write an artist statement says: "My art speaks for itself. I will not kowtow to the dumbing down of contemporary art. My art is my agenda." Art is like politics, business, or love — you can score a lot of integrity points by keeping your mouth shut.

Actress Elizabeth Hurley told an interviewer for Us *magazine that she agreed that Marilyn Monroe was sexy, but she also declared: "I would kill myself if I woke up that fat!" Here, then, are*

9 Better Reasons For Elizabeth Hurley To End Her Life

1. She can't act.

2. Her most successful movie so far is *Austin Powers: International Man of Mystery* — a 98-minute movie which she was in for approximately 19 minutes. She was in the sequel for less than 3 minutes, before the credits, and most of her scenes were done by a stunt double.

3. In England, the British press nicknamed her The Hurl — you figure it out.

4. She produced two films starring her husband Hugh Grant — one, called *Check Him Out!*, was so awful that Disney refused to release it. Her former maid, Alanza Veritero, told *Hello* magazine that Hurley sits up all night drinking red wine, playing *Check Him Out!* over and over again and throwing ashtrays at the screen.

5. Hugh Grant admitted on *The Tonight Show* that he prefers the company of Sunset Boulevard prostitutes because they tell better jokes and are always polite.

6. She once slapped a 4-year-old child actor for forgetting his lines. Hurley later admitted that she "didn't have the best possible childhood either."

7. She tried to have an affair with ED TV co-star Matthew McConaughey. Apparently, Hurley is the only person in Hollywood who doesn't know Matthew McConaughey is gay.

8. She is 33 years old — in Hollywood math, that makes her about 77.

9. Hurley sued the English tabloid *News of the Globe* for describing her as "a boorish, poorly-educated, social climbing, overrated knickers catalogue model gleefully unburdened by talent or style." She lost.

7 Books Every Homosexual Male Must Read

The Fall of the House of Usher
Edgar Allan Poe

Thin, pale, rich and handsome, the eccentric and fidgety Roderick Usher lives unhappily with his reclusive, bed-wetting sister in a big, dark mansion they inherited from their famous and famously crazy family. When Roderick invites his hearty, red-cheeked boyhood "intimate associate" to visit and share the gloom, the two men decide, after much lounging and drinking and poetry reading, that what twitchy Roderick really needs is to stop being so neurotic and aim higher — for total, abject lunacy. If this book is not an allegory for at least three of your worst relationships, I must be projecting.

The Maltese Falcon
Dashiell Hammett

Everybody is greedy and everybody is mean and everybody lies about everything all the time. Sound familiar?

The Terrible Girls
Rebecca Brown

Fags like to make fun of lesbian melodrama — because, of course, fag dramas are all high operas — but isn't it better to learn than to jeer? A tough dyke leant me this book and offered to sever my arms from my shoulders if I lost it. An apt threat 'cause these stories frequently describe acts of dismemberment, disfiguration, dyspepsia and disembowelment. I now understand why women in love often torture each other — because it's fun and they don't have cable. Sisters and brothers, unite!

The Artificial Kingdom
Celeste Olalquiaga
The Manual of Ornament
Richard Glazier

You are gay, therefore you buy a lot of stuff you do not need. Many of these things are what polite people call "interesting" and the rest of us call kitsch. Don't you want to know why you like what you like? I'll tell you why — you're obsessed with your own mortality. You're barricading, stocking your funeral vault, trying to trip up The Grim Reaper, that staunch minimalist. Ornament = longevity.

One Lifetime Is Not Enough
Zsa Zsa Gabor

Zsa Zsa Gabor has been famous for over half a century, and she's done nothing to deserve it. I am paralyzed with insightful envy. And so will you be, especially after you read about the time Mel (or was it Jose? Neither ZZ nor I can remember) Ferrar tossed Zsa Zsa off a Las Vegas hotel balcony and her Balenciaga dress ("so perfectly constructed") popped open like a jellyfish and saved her life. Beats working.

The Complete Saki
Hector Hugh Munro (a.k.a. Saki)

A former Burmese police officer, Miss Munro invented a kind of evil not seen since, well, the occupation of Burma. His smarmy tales of wealthy, lazy, mincing, addle-pated Reginald, Clovis and Comus — three drowned kittens whose only goals in life are to verbally ream each other while molesting the servants — will teach you how to live well in your own bile. It's like *Snippy for Dummies*, without that *dwedful yelwo cahver*.

DESERT STORM II: ORIGINAL MOTION PICTURE SOUNDTRACK

1. *God Bless America*. Celine Dion with The Harlem Boy's Choir. Arranged by David Foster.
2. *Boom! There It Iz! Stealthy Style*. LL Cool J and L'il Kim and L'il Bow Wow.
3. *1991 (we gonna party like it's)*. Prince and the New Power Generation.
4. *Savin' Da World 1 Bitch at a Time*. Tony Bennett and 50 Cent. Recorded live at the Aspen Music Festival.
5. *The Charge of the Light Brigade*. The Boston Pops Orchestra. Narrated by Kevin Costner.
6. *Ahab the Arab (Bag-da-Dad remix)*. Ray Stevens. Remixed by Moby.
7. *Putting Out Fires With Gasoline*. Kid Rock and Pamela Anderson.
8. *Axes to Axis*. Nickleback with James Brown.
9. *Sultans of Schwing! (Love Theme from Desert Storm II)*. Academy of St. Martin's In-The-Fields.
10. *That's What Friends Are For (USA-UK mix)*. Oprah Winfrey and Sarah Ferguson, Duchess of York. Arranged by Quincy Jones.
11. *'Round Midnight at the Oasis*. Mariah Carey and Winton Marsalis.
12. *Over There/I'll Be Seeing You/New York, New York Medley*. Liza Minelli (featuring The New York City Fire Fighters Choir).
13. *God Bless America Muthaf**kah!* Celine Dion and Missy "Misdemeanor" Elliot.

Ontario Family Court: Section 11, Toronto.
Same Sex Marriage Unit (Compensation Division)
The Honourable Justice DJ Jayson-Jay Jacque presiding

July 22, 2017

Marcel Bruce Benderson-Fix v. Lincoln "Bindy" Heloise-Fix

Discovery and Disclosure of Assets

Marcel Bruce Benderson-Fix claims the following items:

- 9 *Queer as Folk* collectable Bobble-Head dolls, 2 autographed. Appraised value of $28,632.
- A signed first edition of the Bruce Weber photography book *He's 13 and Ready for Love*.
- Assorted flatware and 24 place settings from the *Anne-Marie MacDonald At Home* product line.
- A five box CD/DVD/IDV music and interactive vidsensor implant compilation entitled *The Shakira Experience*.
- One feline, short hair Brasilia Rainbow Miniature, male, named Second Mortgage.
- One feline, long hair, unknown parentage, male, named Starter Home.
- Life Member tickets to the Aubergine Ball, the Moss Ball, the Frosted Topaz Ball and the Toronto Fisters and Hand Ballers Tea Dance.
- One personal scalp therapy and physical duress trainer, named Amber-Tsu-Li.
- "Anything bought with my cards."

Lincoln "Bindy" Heloise-Fix claims the following items:

- One faux-fur chest harness and zippered jock strap set (rechargeable).
- One sealed box containing 12 musk scented pillar candles, "acquired" from Ryan Phillippe's Royal York Hotel suite. Sentimental value.
- One Bonobo monkey hide overnight bag with diamante clasp.

- Nova Scotia Plaid-bound 3-volume book set, entitled *Anne-Marie MacDonald's Cherished Recipes from Old Cape Breton*.
- 3 digital video disks, dated 2011, marked: Marcel/Montreal/Sauna de Ganymede.
- Set of five orange glass and petrified cactus wood gilded accent tables purchased at 34th annual Fashion Cares benefit auction. Valued at $11,000. Claimant fully admits that he was inebriated at time of purchase.
- 2-year subscription to the Moisturizer of the Month club.
- Aboriginal status (see attached pp. Govt. of Canada same sex civil union status transference: section 23 C, clause 9).
- "Anything I told him to buy."

Universal Pictures
For Sally McKay

TREE

pearl & olive skinned, grout black at its cloven
base   strung with horned seed fruit the size

of ice cream scoops   scarred pinballs, merry and plentiful as Mexican hatbands
        and as quickly lost

arbutus   you say, and think
            of Arbuckle   poor Fatty   of the many histories of ruined stars   and

stop   at a familiar corner   step off pedals & pinch brake handles   look and glide

over worm white roots teasing water from gravel, from clay
half a block later

GOLDFISH

impatient dart

   slicked with orange vinyl

   enameled feathers, cut to squares   a vellum, feminine wave

soft bullet
there is never enough food
or eyelids for sleep

GERANIUM

a metallic pong
        baby powder, wet dog, Queen Mary Tea and propane

catches deep in the nose   the whiskered strips of cartilage
        toughened by menthol, shit, toaster elements, crotch   off-gassing plastics

but diffuses, turns watery
        and you blink, instead, at that red
            that luxurious paprika over orange over lead grey

a compound glaze   the only colour visible at midnight

FAT MAN

full as a blister
a melon on toothpicks   *tee-hee-hee*

and look! the way his biceps try to bunch, make shapes   but fail, get smothered
    his muscles as taut as a handful of cold cream, as bean curd

look lower, the downy stomach   (pussy willow, rolled sleeping bag)

tee-hee

you begin, drop, start anew   6 sentences, all questions   *why doesn't he*
eat some   wear dark   join a   see a doc   get the staple
                                                              hide?

CAR

bigger than my bedroom, wider than a redwood
The Romper Stomper, The Obeah, Gambol xev, The Magog, L'Embonpoint

is stuck, shuddering   bucking
          a chesty girl in a church parade   tuba in a toilette stall

between two streetcars, two vegetable vans
                  5 bicycles, three Filipino maids chasing
     three blonde tots
     a feral yellow cat (cactus-furred, paper clip skinny & dead
on impact)

6 Poems For Aleister Crowley
For FASTWÜRMS

The Order of the Golden Dawn

Nobody wanted you, Edward Alexander   in 1875, while England peaked
  you, hog nostrils and white veined pate slippery with mother   arrived darkly
  near midnight (so you say)   without bat wings or hail, lightning globes   strange
husbandry between horses and wolves   without props, portents
    but you hardly needed tokens, *Varney the Vampire*'s kit and tackle

You should not have been born, "Alick"   spying your elfin ears, demon pulls
from the mess between her legs   your mother told a Yorkshire midwife, later the world
    there will be a war   ordered the removal of your foreskin (initio) & a bowl
of oolong tea, cooled with hoarfrost   to wash her legs

She was right, of course   At 22, while Europe readied   for unleashed beasts
   you played schisms and sects, laddy heterodoxy   with every occultist south of Wales
       rent The Order you once adored (a secret hive of actors, newspapermen,
parliamentarians & other squawkers)   waged magickal warfare from parlours, solarium
dessert nooks   made notes for *On the Homunculus* (oh, how you wanted one   a satanic
pet a fanged puppy, plumed cat   child with 3 heads)
    shaved your scalp for photographers, became   "the worst young man in England
not hanged"   fought over Nothings

Chogo Ri

Of all his names   Belial, hellspit, faerie, flintspur, swamp-haunt   monster
"mountaineer" is least, yet
Crowley, the Magus of Mayfair   liked to climb

who talks about his bravery at Chogo Ri now? His Himalayan esteem?

Half a century before Sir Edmund, this tool of daemons   spread a blanket
   across a glacier   slept with a dog whip in one hand (for the jumpy porters)
   a Morocco red *grimoire* between his knees (book marked with a sprig
of blue chive, for luck   page 546
 The Calling Forth and Repel of Howler Shades; Called by the Peasantry the names of
Mountain Hags, Snow Incubi, High Ones, etc.)
                lived on air thin as candle light   for 39 days

A rumour:
            at the summit, Crowley pleased himself three times   into a vase
   made of ram bone and faience   found a curling chasm and became husband
to the ice

Did he pray over the pit   bend his frost-blacked fingers into church-and-steeple
   & ask his childhood God for one, please one   can of oil, biscuit, warm boot, map?

I would

LINGAM, OR THE INNER ROBE OF GLORY

"If this secret of sexual magic was perfectly understood . . . nothing which the human imagination can conceive could not be realized"

You never ran out of poetry   for fucking, never stopped ornamenting
the base with the Byzantine, lead with electrum   muck with lilies
    (Collette on Voltaire   "In the end, he was just a dirty little boy
  smelling his fingers")

and so with your cock, that garden gnome   you dressed in abalone cups & threads
spun from rare warbler feathers, strung with sugared peonies & raised to the gods
  who only tittered

but when you made your bed with lady diarists, Oxford math dons   boys
fond of birch rod   did you once call a lay a lay?
Change, in the quiet behind canopies, "ruby star of Isis" to plain *cunt*   "wand of Delphi"
to *little man*   bend over, shut up and take it?

THE BOOK OF THE HEART GIRT WITH A SERPENT

Another *Holy Book* (italics His)   costing 3 days
     of rhymes and exclamations, Sufi sacraments and penile tricks   showy adjectives
stolen from the ancients, from Viennese newspapers   a pocket volume attending
every purpled concern of the perfumed classes

met with shrugs

His fondest subscribers, satiated with pronouncements   weekly Wondrous Advisories
of Imminent New Dawns   fed too long on sherry banquets and limp orgies staged
in ruined languages   on tin swords & 5 edge stars made of penny candles
        butchers' blood anticlimaxes

neglected to renew

Can a fool lie?
No   He can write poetry

The Book of the Law

Cairo, 1904

Perdurabo (Crawley, in incarnation   tonsured in white tails, a supper club
   Dr. Strange   cutting his meat with an emerald dagger)
accepts a vision:
         a flying gold lamp   8 glass hammers, 3 peacock leather volumes afloat   a scented
code, the final Book of Antioch (choose your angel)   a gin dream
      "a million times more important than the discovery of the Wheel"
but hardly as comprehensible

'Tis the *Key of Progress*   he boasted, then fled
   for New York, books at the printers   accepted the toasts of widowers bored
by rap-and-tambourine mediums, heiresses keen for Yahweh   slumming
Knickerbocker stoics and Kaiser apologists (later Nazis)
looking for blank slates

Do What Thou Wilt

December 1, 1947   Death

"Men worship only their own weaknesses personified"   you dictated
  from your Celafu *chambre*   (a 7-walled, fly-smeared Lake Country decorator's
wonderland, a house of Oriental ornaments, sable blankets   *petits annonces diaboliques*
& bad art)

and meant, only   listen to me   *me*
The Beast, El Haji, The White Adept, breeder of The Crowned Child (a girl
one Lola Zaza, awkward and quickly forgotten   bequeathed 300 quid for clothing)

you, who took communion with creatures not named by God   Aiwaz, Baphomet
Iamblichus   with Tengchong mendicants and Minnesota covens   who drank semen
with Yeats and unnamed New Orleans Negro poets

you, the numerologist who bounced cheques   herald without horn, Sunday supplement
or broadcast coloratura

to me, please   you begged, meaning
only a cup of water   & all the world

London After Midnight
For James BL Hollands

The Quebec, Old Quebec Street

Is not burdened by le québécois
   by loud silks & Birk's jewelry, Celine drag & hissing, hoe-nosed boys who smell
of lemon and milk   of gamy Mountain Ash in flower   of semen dosed
with molasses sugar, stale bean curd   all the off-gasses of disfavour
       Not even a stray Belgian, Cameroonian, or Acadian has pissed here
because this is England   place names are decorative

A man tickles my elbow   Reggie, red-bristled and faint-voiced   a *slinker*, I'm told
(and don't understand)   a man made of gardeners' wire and press board   but cheaper
than both   a stew chicken marinated in Shea butter   in cigarettes, hand creams,
wallpaper glue, standing black water and keen class analysis (his birthright)

Drinks come, Reggie pays (a nine-eyed boy dowager in her corner berth audibly blisters
from shock)   tips his glass against his forehead, a goat mauling a can: *Me mum,*
see, she left me proper dead rich   didn't she?
   a patent question, the British Double Interrogative   with so many answers
all of them rude

The King's Arms Pub, Poland Street

Founded by Druids in 1238   or naturalists, or sodomite pagans, or merchant pederasts
with land and income enough for arbors, hiding places (nobody knows the entire story,
as Lord Aitken said of British history)   no king would slake here, take the waters

where jellied men perch topsy-turvy, shins to carpet, on low footstools   dainty as forklifts
& a Spanish teen, thinner than stemware, whispers *I like you   yes how you say? With
me*   to London's drunkest two hundred and seventy pound toiletries clerk

where the piss stalls bulge, belly to belly   with gay fathers and Lulu fans run to fat
     to auntish winks, barley-stuck kisses, garden chat, menthol cheroots, Dockers &
URLs   to PoshandBecks, *Footballer's Wives*, George Michael, footy,
Kylie Minogue, footy, Lonsdale of London, civil unions & luvy-sweety-deary-mate
  to buttoned jumpers, footy, Graham Norton, tandoori & Damien Hirst   to brown sauce
on eggs, M&S take away, *The Daily Telegraph*, poor old Morrisey and more, more
forever & always Princess fucking Diana   shabby queen

THE HOIST, SOUTH LAMBETH ROAD

Follow the path south   cross west at Vauxhall, walk over a buried river
up metal stairs, down again (mind the rust)   slip under
        the white brick arch, dust the lime off your shoes
    check for hooligans   then   *run*
        past the Somali cleaning ladies, sleepy design students, pinstriped oafs who smell
of ass and lime-zest Speedstick
        duck the murderous A34!
            run fast   through a fusty, dripping tunnel   made of moss and black gull feathers
to a low light bulb behind an inset gate, mesh and bars
to the double guarded, camera swept, urine salted front porch
of the world's most over-publicized leather bar

Inside, a bored weightlifter snap curls a clipboard, pats his pectorals & flashes a torch
    over my inseam and down, police style
        to my shoes

brown, my shoes are brown!   he scowls, brown . . . might as well be ballet slippers
brown shoes are Sundays only . . .

Now, everything's in jeopardy — Babylon is shut, Xanadu closed for renovations —
I'll miss the fisting platform, the St. Andrew's cross, the rubber sling, the glory hole
lattice, the allegedly insatiable Dutch tourists   boot night, uniform night,
squaddie social, headmaster's meet and greet, rodeo romp, sport kit klatch, "pits and
cracks" and "jocks and socks"

        5 pounds extra for brown shoes, mate   I sigh, pay, cross the hell mouth
and wipe my glasses

6 men, 4 of them seniors, singing along to Justin Timberlake
décor copied from *Stomp!*
    the bartender's flip flops squeak in the damp   like old church pews

THE STAG, BRESSENDEN PLACE

Shapely and fresh as a wheel of graying curd
a former sheep-cote-in-the-round (ovine panopticon?)   spared in the Blitz
by three Luftwaffe fags with menace in their hearts   "It will do more damage
standing," the oldest shrieked
      The Stag is the Tuesday pick of London's disappointed class

of dumpy church wardens, carping lesbian trench sweeps, *Railway Children* enthusiasts
ska revivalists   six drunks back from the dog races, the Sugar Beet Board payroll master
      a bearded, sooty, ancient Victoria and Albert Museum archivist dressed in a fawn
blazer, blue shirt, rust tie and knee-high handkerchief skirt

      & Christopher, blonde Liberal Democrat   city councilor, manor kept war
apologist

Our goal in Iraq   is the exportation of British good will

such as this place

THE ADMIRAL DUNCAN, OLD COMPTON STREET

Cannot be mentioned without talk of bombs, enjoyed without pause   memorial
breaths   I forget, was it fertilizer, dynamite or *plastique* in 1999   pipe or parcel
    larded with nails   razors   ball bearings
(curse amulets)   christians or muslims or nazis   the mafia, random discontent
perhaps a boy from the Cotswolds who made no friends in Soho   maybe a village idiot
    a man chased by bugs, flus, endless colds, hives & shingles   his grieving mother
(is anyone simply insane anymore?)   some kids, some brats, just some bad kids

who did this, who blew open this weary & indifferent local   this public house

now stocked with videocams, purse-checkers, barmen trained in ju-jitsu   guarded
drinkers   afraid of firecrackers, popped balloons?

XXL, London Bridge Arches, Southwark Street

Only Londoners would eat themselves
into fashion   dedicate a city season to rolls, back fat, plum teats, 4 stone
guts   make gay the animal names body fat conjures (bear, panda, cub, badger, bull, pig,
sloth)   "discover" centuries after the Arabs, Malaysians, West Indians & Prussians
how fat men like to fuck

in blacked out, angular ballrooms   where even the heftiest Twickenham chips gorgers,
floor-benders and chair leg challengers   can be cornered   we group, make mobs
of indulgence   pat our stomachs, another's   open our buttery legs, so unused to air
to attention   shoot sugary semen into mouths crusted with lager and cakes
forgetting diabetes, early insulin resistance syndrome   herniated discs & shin splints
gout & rashes & chafing & taunts   self-hatred and the first rule
of English foppery   *eat nothing*